ISBN 978-1-5284-1586-6
PIBN 10273533

1 MONTH OF
FREE
READING

at
www.ForgottenBooks.com

By purchasing this book you are eligible for one month membership to ForgottenBooks.com, giving you unlimited access to our entire collection of over 1,000,000 titles via our web site and mobile apps.

To claim your free month visit:

www.forgottenbooks.com/free273533

English
Français
Deutsche
Italiano
Español
Português

www.forgottenbooks.com

Mythology Photography **Fiction**
Fishing Christianity **Art** Cooking
Essays Buddhism Freemasonry
Medicine **Biology** Music **Ancient
Egypt** Evolution Carpentry Physics
Dance Geology **Mathematics** Fitness
Shakespeare **Folklore** Yoga Marketing
Confidence Immortality Biographies
Poetry **Psychology** Witchcraft
Electronics Chemistry History **Law**
Accounting **Philosophy** Anthropology
Alchemy Drama Quantum Mechanics
Atheism Sexual Health **Ancient History**
Entrepreneurship Languages Sport
Paleontology Needlework Islam
Metaphysics Investment Archaeology
Parenting Statistics Criminology
Motivational

TARIFF SCHEDULES

HEARINGS

BEFORE THE

U.S.

COMMITTEE ON WAYS AND MEANS

HOUSE OF REPRESENTATIVES

ON

SCHEDULE E—SUGAR, MOLASSES, AND MANUFACTURES OF

JANUARY 15, 1913

TESTIMONY OF

FRANK C. LOWRY
OF NEW YORK

WASHINGTON
GOVERNMENT PRINTING OFFICE
1913

CANE SUGAR, ETC.

TESTIMONY OF FRANK C. LOWRY, NEW YORK.

[Representing the Federal Sugar Refining Co., of New York, and the Committee of Wholesale Grocers, formed to assist in obtaining cheaper sugars for consumers through the reduction of duties on raw and refined sugars.]

Mr. LOWRY. Mr. Chairman and gentlemen of the committee, I represent the Federal Sugar Refining Co., of New York, and the committee of wholesale grocers, formed about four years ago to assist in obtaining cheaper sugars for consumers through the reduction of duties on raw and refined sugars.

I fully appreciate that, so far as the tariff on sugar is concerned, little can be added to the information which is already a matter of public record, and at the disposal of the committee. Consequently, anything that is said at these hearings must necessarily be in the way of repetition.

I would first like to call the committee's attention to the fact that the United States is not dependent for its supply of sugar upon "foreign countries," in the general acceptance of this term. The consumption of sugar in the United States for 1912, according to Messrs. Willett & Gray, was 3,504,182 long tons. The estimates for the following crops of 1912–13 are:

	Long tons.
Cuba	2,328,000
Louisiana (1912)	160,000
Texas	10,000
Porto Rico	340,000
Hawaiian Islands	500,000
Philippine Islands	200,000
Domestic beet	625,000
Total	4,163,000

By this it will be seen that the production of sugar inside our tariff wall more than equals consumption. All of these producers have the advantage of the full height of our tariff wall with the exception of Cuba, which is inside this wall to the extent of the 20 per cent reduction, as a result of the reciprocity treaty of 1903. This island, adjacent to our shores, with interests so closely allied to those of the United States, has been favorably equipped by nature for the economical production of sugar and is able and willing to supply the United States with this sugar at a low cost if it were not for the high tariff which enhances the price. The testimony before this and the Hardwick committee has clearly shown that the domestic producer's price is always based on the in-bond value of foreign sugars plus the duty and cost of refining. In addition to these charges, the beet-sugar factories add the freight from New York or San Francisco to

3

distributing market as well. In the sale of the domestic producer's product, the cost of production has no relation to the selling price. We have a clear example of this in the price of sugar in our Western States. Take January 6 as an example, and we find the following quotations made by the cane refiners and beet factories:

New York City:	Cents.
Cane	4. 65–4. 70
Colorado beet	4. 60
San Francisco:	
Cane	5. 20
Beet	5. 00
Denver, Colo.:	
Cane	5. 50
Beet	5. 20
Chicago:	
Cane (New York and San Francisco, refined)	4. 885
Beet	4. 735

At this point I would call your attention to the manner in which the New York price for refined sugar is arrived at:

	Cents.
Raw sugars now being received from Cuba cost refiners, basis 96 test, cost and freight, not less than	2. 375
Insurance, one-half per cent, or	.012
Duty	1. 348
Refiners' first cost, duty paid	3. 74

Deducting the usual discount of 2 per cent from their price of 4.65 cents on refined, this leaves a margin to cover the cost of refining, packing, and marketing of the difference between 4.56 cents and 3.74 cents, or

	.82
The average margin for seven years is	.859

After these deductions have been made anything that is left is profit.

This calculation indicates that the price to the American consumer is being affected only to the extent of the tariff charged on Cuban sugars, and while this is true at the present time, when there is great pressure to sell in Cuba, it is not always the case, and during October, November, and part of December, 1912, sugar paying the Cuban rate of duty, free sugar, and sugar paying the full rate of duty were being sold at the same duty-paid equivalent. During this period the price to the consumer was affected to the full height of our tariff wall. I cover this point more fully in my brief under the heading "The effect of our tariff wall and Cuban reciprocity."

That, I think, shows you that the domestic producer bases his price on the New York price plus freight to interior markets, and the New York price is based on the foreign price, plus the duty.

The trade will not pay the same price for beet as for cane sugar, which accounts for the differential.

Notwithstanding the fact that all the sugar used in our Western States is of domestic production, either being Hawaiian cane or domestic beet, and pays no duty, the price is always higher than in the East, where the sugar imported pays a high duty. As a result of the tariff the consumers in these Western States are receiving no benefit whatever from the fact that in their immediate locality refined sugar is being produced at a cost of around 3 cents a pound; the price only recedes as we approach the eastern coast, where the domestic producers come into competition with the refiners using imported sugar. The lowest price for sugar in the United States is in New York.

Let us now see how the price for sugar to the American consumer is affected by the duty. Taking the figures of the Department of Commerce and Labor, Bureau of Statistics, No. 240, page 517, we find the average cost per pound, free on board in foreign countries, of the raw sugar imported from 1905 to 1911, inclusive, was 2.378 cents per pound. To this we must add the freight to get the cost laid down at United States ports, say, 0.14 cent, making the in-bond price of this sugar at United States ports 2.518 cents. During these seven years the margin between the price paid by refiners for their raw material and their selling price on refined has been 0.859 cent per pound. Had refiners not been required to pay any duty on this sugar, and this margin were added to the in-bond price of the raw material, it would have made the average selling price for these seven years 3.377 cents per pound. Messrs. Willett & Gray show that the average refiner's price, free on board New York, for these years was 4.98 cents per pound, showing clearly that, as a result of the tariff, the price was increased to the extent of 1.603 cents per pound. We can therefore take this figure as a fair indication of the indirect bounty that has been paid to the domestic sugar industry during these years. To give you an idea of what this amounted to, I would call your attention to the fact that, based on the consumption, during this period the American people have been required to pay $776,867,000 more for their sugar than they would have paid under free sugar. For this period the total value of the domestic beet and Louisiana cane sugar produced was less than $500,000,000.

During these seven years the Government collected in revenue from sugar the following amounts:

	Revenue.	Consumption.
		Long tons.
1905	$51,171,283	2,632,216
1906	52,440,228	2,864,013
1907	60,135,181	2,993,979
1908	49,984,905	3,185,789
1909	56,213,472	3,257,060
1910	52,810,995	3,350,255
1911	52,496,559	3,351,388

It has been said that the tariff on sugar is a revenue measure, but, strictly speaking, this is not a fact. The Government now receives revenue from only about 50 per cent of the sugar that we consume. If we are to tax sugar for the purpose of producing revenue, then we should adopt the method employed by all of the principal countries of Europe and require all the sugar consumed to share in producing this revenue. This has been done by the application of what is known as a "consumption tax," which is paid on all sugars, whether of foreign or domestic origin. Under this method our refiners of both beet and cane sugar would be required to pay a tax of so much per hundred pounds on the amount of sugar they produced, but there need be no taxes on raw sugars made in our insular possessions—Porto Rico, Hawaii, and the Philippines—or in Louisiana, as the tax on these sugars would be paid by refiners before they were put on the market. It would be necessary, however, to have a provision in the law that any refined sugar they might make or any raw sugar imported from any source for direct consumption would have to pay the " consumption tax " before the sugar could be sold to the trade. In this way, by taxing all sugar consumed, say, 25 cents a hundred, the same amount of revenue can be raised for the Government as would be derived under an import rate of 50 cents a hundred on half the sugar consumed. It has the added advantage of only advancing the price to the consumer 25 cents a hundred instead of 50 cents, and increases as consumption increases. You will note that under the present arrangement the Government derived little more revenue from sugar in 1911 than in 1906, although consumption increased 17 per cent. I believe this demonstrates that from a purely revenue standpoint the present method of collecting revenue from sugar is faulty.

The beneficiaries of our high tariff on sugar are loud in their clamor that the present rate should be maintained for the purpose of revenue; in the next breath they make the claim that it will not be long before all the sugar which we consume will be of domestic origin, and overlook the fact that in this event the Government will receive no revenue at all from the tariff on imported sugar; so it is clear that they are not so much concerned about Uncle Sam's pocketbook as they are about their own.

Let us consider the domestic sugar producer's position. It is not my understanding that the people of the United States desire to be heavily taxed so that the sugar producers in Porto Rico, Hawaii, or the Philippines can make excessive profits.

If protection to infant industries were needed, it has been given. Porto Rico and Hawaii have practically reached their maximum production, all available cane lands now being under cultivation, so that little further progress can be made, with the possible exception of improvements in yields and efficiency in the mills. Both of these islands have, in the past, worked successfully under conditions of absolute free trade. Hawaii boasts, and with reason, that the industry is run under more scientific conditions than any other sugar industry in the world. It was currently reported that the Hawaiian crop of 1911 was sold for about $52,000,000, with the planters' profits $20,000,000. I have not been able to ascertain what the profits were in 1912, but under date of November 21, 1912, the Kekahala mill declared a dividend of 87½ per cent.

I do not believe that the American people should be heavily taxed so as to produce these results.

Let us now consider Louisiana's position. This " infant industry " is over 100 years old and has always been directly or indirectly subsidized. In 1894–95 it produced 316,000 long tons; in 1911, 315,000 long tons, and the average for the last seven years is 316,500 tons.

Louisiana has in the past contended that it cost them on the average 3¾ cents per pound to produce raw sugar. In this statement they present the strongest possible indictment that can be drawn against their industry, as they clearly show that with Cuba, Porto Rico, and Hawaii producing the same grade of raw sugar at around 2 cents a pound the Louisiana industry is a highly artificial one.

I do not, however, think this cost should be taken seriously, as it appears the cost in good, bad, and indifferent factories was taken and averaged, without taking any standard as a basis for arriving at a proper cost, and their view seems to be the same as that taken by the beet-sugar factories, namely, that the higher they can make their cost appear, the higher you must make the tariff bounty. I believe that closer investigation will show that the most slipshod methods are employed in many of the Louisiana mills, and consequently any returns made from them should be ignored.

However, it is clear that this heavy indirect subsidy granted to the Louisiana industry by the United States Government has not tended to produce the best results. Messrs. Willett & Gray are the authority for the statement that there are now 210 mills in the State of Louisiana, of which 32 are the old open-kettle style of factory. So we find Louisiana, with 210 factories, producing 316,000 long tons of sugar, as compared with Cuba, with 174 mills, producing 2,328,000 long tons, and Porto Rico, with about 43 mills, producing 340,000 long tons.

These figures make it clear that, aside from all other reasons, the cost of producing sugar in Louisiana must necessarily be very high. But the happy-go-lucky methods of the Louisiana planter have not been the only, or even the most serious, handicap with which the industry has had to contend. Nature herself rebels against any attempt to grow cane sugar, a tropical plant, in a temperate climate. The constant fear of frost requires the cutting of the cane in October before it is properly matured and the result is that the cane yields only from 6 to 7 per cent, as compared with 10 to 11 per cent in Cuba, with an occasional yield of 14 per cent, and 14 to 15 per cent in Hawaii.

After 100 years' work, Louisiana, under unnatural conditions, but with a heavy subsidy as an offset, managed to produce 316,000 long tons, while Cuba, under natural conditions and without subsidy, increases its crop in one year over 425,000 long tons. If a clear example were needed of the fallacy of attempting to foster an industry under unnatural conditions, we have it in Louisiana. One constantly hears that the sugar industry is a detriment to the State, and if the people would only give it up and devote themselves to the cultivation of other crops for which nature has especially favorably endowed them, all would be on a much better footing.

The industry has had its chance. Those engaged in it have had practically everything they wanted in the way of Government help, and they have no further claim on the American people if to-day they find themselves unable to meet their competitors, who are producing raw sugar under natural conditions at a cost of around 2 cents per pound and refined beet sugar at a cost of around 3 cents per pound.

I do not understand it to be the wish of the American people that an illegitimate industry be subsidized through the tariff.

The tariff, in its relation to the beet-sugar industry, is not nearly so complicated as the beneficiaries of the present tariff try to make it appear.

The industry is divided into two parts, agricultural and manufacturing. The beet-sugar factories themselves recognize that the farmer who grows sugar beets does not require a high protective tariff, and they pay no more—and, if anything, less—for sugar beets than is paid by the factories in Germany, where the protective-tariff rate is only 52 cents per hundred on refined and 47 cents on raw, as compared with our rate of $1.90 on refined, $1.685 on full-duty-paying raw sugars and $1.348 on Cubas.

They have presented ample evidence tending to show that the farmer is well satisfied with his present position; so that all the testimony that the representatives of the beet-sugar factories give to show how the farming industry will suffer if the tariff is reduced is put forth with a view of diverting your attention. You will hear a great deal about the farmers' indirect benefits, and you will note in their arguments the beet-sugar factories conveniently appropriate for themselves all the benefits to the farmer which come from "intensive" instead of "extensive" cultivation of the soil. They will compare the cereal and grain yields of the United States with crops of Continental Europe and claim that the high figures of the latter are due entirely to the cultivation of the sugar beet. They will avoid telling you that in England, where sugar beets are not grown, the yields of these other crops compare favorably with continental yields, as this would prove conclusively that it was the manner of farming and not the sugar beets that was responsible for these results. Taking the other side of the question, we find that sugar-beet yields in the United States are nearly the same (some localities exceed) as in Germany, so that in this particular we are closer to the foreign yield than we are on cereals and grains. This would, of course, mean that less protection was needed by the farmer on sugar beets than on these other crops. All this, however, is aside from the issue; i. e., as the farmer now receives no benefit from our high tariff on sugar, he therefore should not be handicapped by its removal. I would also mention that even the stand-pat element of the Republican Party recognized that from an agricultural point of view no protection is necessary, as sugar-beet seed is admitted free of duty, and sugar beets (which are the product of the farm) pay only a nominal rate of 10 per cent. This, on the beets imported, is equivalent to 0.14 cent per pound of sugar, based on the sugar content.

Having found that the agricultural phase of this business does not benefit from the present high tariff, let us now consider the beet-sugar factory's position.

I have never heard the contention made that a well-equipped beet-sugar factory in the United States could not operate as cheaply as anywhere else in the world. The cost of labor does not enter to any extent into the factory's cost of operation. One frequently hears the claim that beet sugar must be very pure, because it is not touched by a single human hand from the time the beets enter at one side of the factory until refined sugar is ready for delivery at the other side. So it is clear that the cost of labor does not play an important part in their process of manufacture. You will find in all their statements that the beet-sugar men confine their comparisons to statements along the following line: " We must have a high tariff because we pay our watchman $2 a day and in Germany he receives only 50 cents." This is immaterial; it is the labor cost per pound of sugar produced that counts. This does not exceed 0.14 cent per pound.

Fuel is an important item, and this, of course, is cheaper in the United States than abroad, particularly in our Western States, where oil is used. It is a well-recognized fact in the manufacturing business that the larger the production in a factory the lower the cost per unit, and the factories in the United States average considerably larger than those abroad.

The investigations of the Hardwick committee proved what everyone in the sugar business knew—that the tariff on sugar has in the past served the purpose of enabling those engaged in the domestic beet-sugar industry to overcapitalize their plants and to pay excessive dividends on watered stock. As an indication of how these interests have capitalized the tariff, I would call your attention to the fact that the combined capitalization of the beet-sugar plants in the United States is now $141,000,000, and these plants, working 3 months in the year, produce 625,000 long tons of sugar, while cane-sugar refiners, with approximately $110,000,000 invested in refining, working 12 months in the year, produce 2,900,000 long tons.

In closing I would like to call your attention to the fact that even the stand-pat element in the Republican Party has admitted that the present tariff on sugar is indefensible. So all are agreed that some reduction must be made, and the question to be decided is how much, if any, of the present tariff should be retained?

If you find it impossible to place sugar on the free list, I urge you to consider as a maximum rate the rate I recommended to the Finance Committee, 62 cents per 100 pounds on refined sugar and 60 cents on raw sugar testing 96°, with the assessed differential per degree of 0.006 cent per pound. Importations from Cuba would, under our reciprocity treaty, pay 20 per cent less than these rates, and as a result of this rate the price of refined sugar to the consumer would probably be advanced by the duty about 53 cents per 100 pounds instead of $1.60, as at present.

Be assured that any sugar industry that can not work profitably with a protection of half a cent a pound (this being 20 per cent to 25 per cent of the cost of production under natural conditions) is artificial in the extreme.

Sugar is a large business, and the margin of profit should be small in it and depending upon volume of business to carry you through.

Mr. HARRISON. This is the protective rate suggested by you?

Mr. LOWRY. Yes.

Mr. HARRISON. You do not refer to the present rate?

Mr. LOWRY. No. I am comparing the present "pork-barrel" protective tariff with a scientific protective tariff. This rate I suggest is a trifle higher than the rate which the countries of Europe have arrived at as a proper protective rate. This is purely from a protective standpoint, you understand.

I would call your attention to the fact that this protective rate is a trifle higher than that which the leading countries of Europe (where beet sugar is produced so extensively) have decided is a proper protective tariff. The rate of 0.47 cent on raw and 0.52 cent on refined was agreed upon at the convention of a number of countries of Europe, known as the Brussels Convention, and was adopted by Austria, Belgium, France, and Germany as a maximum protective rate to be charged. This is, perhaps, the nearest approach we have to a scientific conclusion as to what is a proper protective tariff for the beet-sugar industry. No evidence has been presented to show that on a protective basis this rate could not be adopted by the United States to advantage. I would also call your attention to the fact that, based on the inbond price of sugar for the past seven years of 2.518 cents per pound, this tariff would be equivalent to an ad valorem rate of about 21 per cent and would produce $19,330,000 in annual revenue, would subsidize the domestic sugar industry to a like amount, $19,330,000, and would result in a yearly saving on our present consumption of $83,988,234 to the American consumers.

It seems to me that in producing this much revenue a necessity of life, like sugar, is doing its full share, but if you should decide that sugar must produce more revenue, then I urge you to adopt in addition the consumption tax, which is strictly a revenue measure.

Mr. SHACKLEFORD. As a revenue tax it would be paid by the consumer?

Mr. LOWRY. Oh, yes; just as the tariff tax is now paid by the consumer. You can not get revenue without having it paid by the consumer, I believe. The difference is if you tax all the sugars 25 cents a hundred pounds you get the same amount of revenue that you would get by taxing half the sugar consumed, or that which is imported, at the rate of 50 cents a hundred pounds. The former method has the advantage of increasing the price to the consumer only a quarter of a cent a pound, while the latter increases the price a half a cent a pound.

Mr. SHACKLEFORD. Is it an example that might become contagious?

Mr. LOWRY. In what way?

Mr. SHACKLEFORD. As a means of taxing other domestic products.

Mr. LOWRY. If it reduced the price it might be an advantage to do that. I do not know whether it would become contagious or not.

Mr. PAYNE. That chance for contagion has had about 100 years to work, has it not?

Mr. LOWRY. What did you say?

Mr. PAYNE. That chance for contagion with other products has had about 100 years to work, has it not?

Mr. LOWRY. As I do not believe it to be the sentiment of our people that American industries should be compelled to compete with bounty-fed products of other nations, I would suggest that, whether or not sugar be placed on the free list, a countervailing-duty clause be enacted similar to that found in the tariff law of 1909, section 6, page 84.

Gentlemen, the United States, because of its proximity to Cuba and its insular possessions—Porto Rico, Hawaii, and the Philippines—as well as from the fact that beet sugar can be produced in our Western States at a very low cost, should have cheaper sugar than any nation in the world. From these sources, with their natural advantages, we are assured not only of an ample supply of sugar, but that this supply could be obtained at a minimum cost if it were not for the high duty which enhances the price.

No other nation in the world is so favorably situated, and the question is, Are the people to receive the benefit of our natural advantages, or are they to be exploited for the benefit of the promoters of our domestic beet and cane sugar industry? The present high tariff means the latter.

Mr. Lowry. There has been some question raised by the domestic sugar industry as to a reduction in the tariff going to the consumer of articles wherein sugar was used in manufacture. Condensed milk was one of the points which they raised, and I made some inquiries on that question. It did not seem to me possible if you reduced the manufacturer's first cost that competition would not take care of a reduction in the sale price of his finished product. So, as I started out to say, I made some inquiries of condensed-milk manufacturers, and the conclusion is—well, I will read this:

PHILADELPHIA, November 27, 1912.

Mr. F. C. Lowry,
Secretary and Treasurer, No. 138 Front Street, New York City.

DEAR SIR: Replying to yours of November 26, we beg to advise that approximately 17 pounds of refined sugar enters into the manufacture of an average case of condensed milk. This, figured at 1⅝ cents per pound, increases the cost of condensed milk per case by 27⅝ cents. There are 48 cans to a case, and the cost to the manufacturer is therefore increased by more than one-half cent per can. This one-half cent could be saved to consumers were the sugar duty abolished.

Yours, very truly,

HIRES CONDENSED MILK CO.,
H. C. HOOKS, Secretary.

Mr. Lowry. This one-half cent per can could be saved to the consumer in the case of the condensed milk.

I also made some inquiries of candy manufacturers and found those who handled bulk candies were in favor of free sugar or a material reduction in the present rate of duty, while those who handled package goods were not so keen for it. I did not understand that at first, and finally when I put it up to them they said:

Well, our industry is at present standardized. We have certain sizes of packages all through the industry, we will say, to sell for 5 cents or 10 cents or some other sum. If you reduce the price of sugar we will have to give a larger package for 5 cents or give a present 5-cent package for less money. That would mean a reorganization of our business and a lot of trouble.

From this you will readily see that the consumer would get the benefit from a reduction in duty.

Now, gentlemen of the committee, I believe what I have said pretty well covers the situation, taken together with the papers I have handed the reporter. If you would like me to review the matter further I can do so, or if you wish to ask any questions I will be glad to answer them.

Mr. FORDNEY. Mr. Chairman, I would like to ask the gentleman a few questions.

The CHAIRMAN. All right, Mr. Fordney, you may proceed.

Mr. FORDNEY. Mr. Lowry, you have stated that the list prices for sugar in this country is based upon the rates for sugar in New York?

Mr. LOWRY. Yes, sir.

Mr. FORDNEY. Was that true during 1911?

Mr. LOWRY. In the main it was. There might have been a particular period when it was not, but—yes; I guess it was.

Mr. FORDNEY. There was a very particular period. Is this not true, that an abundance of testimony was furnished before the special committee on the investigation of the American Sugar Refining Co., known as the Hardwick committee, that after domestic sugar was off the market in June the refiners in New York put up the price of sugar to as high as 7.5 cents per pound, and that continued during July, August, and September?

Mr. Lowry. There was ample testimony to show——

Mr. Fordney (interposing). Is it not true whether there was testimony to that effect or not?

Mr. Lowry. Domestic sugars, in the first place, came on the market in the latter part of August of that year.

Mr. Fordney. No; wait a minute and answer the question I propounded. Let us see if we can not get at this right. Is it not true that the price of sugar in New York advanced during July, August, and September to as high as $7.50 per hundred pounds?

Mr. Lowry. Yes; for a short period it is.

Mr. Fordney. Oh, for a short period, you say. Was it not for three or four months?

Mr. Lowry. No; it started to advance on the 5th day of July from 5 cents.

Mr. Fordney. Mr. Lowry, is not this true, that in October, when domestic beet sugar came on the market, your company, the Federal Sugar Refining Co., dropped its price from about 7¼ cents per pound to 5.75 cents er pound when the beet sugar was put on the market at 5.55 cents?

Mr. Lowry. No; beet sugar was put on the market the latter part of August, coming on from California. California beet sugar was sold very late in August that year.

Mr. Fordney. There is no beet sugar made——

Mr. Lowry (interposing). Of course, Mr. Fordney, if you just pick out particular dates——

Mr. Fordney (interposing). There was no beet sugar made in August and put on the market in the Eastern States?

Mr. Lowry. There was in California.

Mr. Fordney. I mean in New York.

Mr. Lowry. California produces a great deal more sugar than they use there and it is shipped East.

Mr. Fordney. Mr. Chairman, I appeal to you that the gentleman is avoiding answers to my questions and making an argument. He has already had full time in which to make his argument, and I want him to answer my questions now, if he will.

The Chairman. Mr. Lowry, you will please answer Mr. Fordney's questions. You have the privilege of answering the questions in your own way, but please try to answer his questions.

Mr. Lowry. I will.

Mr. Fordney. Is it not true that after domestic beet sugar was off the market in 1911 the refiners of sugar advanced the price as high as $7.50 per hundred pounds in New York?

Mr. Lowry. No; the big advance began in July, and culminated in September and October, when the new crop of sugar in Europe came on the market. They advanced refined sugar as raw sugar advanced, as the world's values advanced.

Mr. Fordney. Well, I will get to that in just a minute. I want to know about this now.

Mr. Lowry. All right.

Mr. Fordney. Is it not true that when beet sugar came on the market your price dropped abnormally; I mean, the price at which your company sold sugars for in the New York market?

Mr. Lowry. Beet sugars were on the market during the whole period.

Mr. FORDNEY. No; they were not. I beg to differ with you.

Mr. LOWRY. Suppose I quote some prices or put them in the record? We have had some correspondence on the subject, and this paper covers the thing clearly, and I will just put in the whole record:

COMMITTEE OF WHOLESALE GROCERS,
New York, January 18, 1912.

DEAR SIR: Knowing that you are interested in the tariff on sugar, I would like to give you an idea of the extremes to which the domestic industry will go in order to have the Government maintain the present high tariff rate, which grants such a heavy subsidy to this industry.

Mr. Frederic R. Hathaway, of the Michigan Beet Sugar Co., prepared an affidavit, which the Hon. J. W. Fordney, Congressman from Michigan, and member of the Hardwick investigating committee, filed with the committee on December 6. Mr. Hathaway's affidavit shows the price quoted by the various New York refiners from September 1 to November 20, ranging from 6.25 to 7.50 cents. The price quoted by the Michigan Sugar Co. on the same dates is not given. He goes on to state that the "Michigan Beet Sugar Co. began delivery of this season's sugar on October 12, 1911; that up to and including November 18, 1911, it had invoiced 860 cars of sugar," and concludes with the following statement: "Deponent further states that of the total amount of sugar invoiced by the Michigan Beet Sugar Co., as above stated, from October 12 to November 18, A. D. 1911, 94.1 per cent was invoiced on the basis of $5.55 per hundred pounds, or 5.55 cents per pound." The purpose of this affidavit is to have the uninitiated believe that the Michigan Sugar Co. assumed a charitable rôle this year and sold their sugar at a relatively lower price than that quoted by the New York cane-sugar refiners. In other words, that during the recent spectacular advance in sugar, the domestic sugar industry stepped into the breach and "saved the day" by selling sugar to consumers at a concession, thereby protecting them from the "extortion" of the New York refiners.

The attitude assumed by them is perhaps best shown in the testimony of the writer before the Hardwick committee last December when being questioned by Mr. J. W. Fordney, of Michigan, the champion in the House of Representatives of the beet-sugar industry (p. 3362):

Mr. FORDNEY. What justified you, your firm, in selling September sugar at 7.25 cents per pound, when the domestic industry shortly afterwards, as soon as their sugar began to go on the market, sold for 5.55? What caused you to come down on the price?

Mr. LOWRY. They sold for what?

Mr. FORDNEY. 5.55.

Mr. LOWRY. Do you not know that the domestic industry was at that time quoting 6.50 cents a pounds?

Mr. FORDNEY. No.

Mr. LOWRY. I know that it was.

Mr. FORDNEY. I put an affidavit in the record on that.

Mr. LOWRY. Well. * * *

Mr. FORDNEY. They had no sugar in the market in September. They had none until their season opened, on October 12, and they began selling at 5.55 f. o. b. factory.

Mr. LOWRY. And when did they begin selling at 5.55?

Mr. FORDNEY. As soon as the season opened.

Mr. LOWRY. Not at all. They began when cane sugars were selling at 5.65.

Mr. FORDNEY. I beg your pardon. I looked up the records themselves, the bill books and the invoices, and on October 12, when the season opened, they quoted sugar at 5.55 and sold it at that, and continued to sell. They sold 809 carloads out of about 850 carloads at that price, 5.55, while your firm was selling at 7.25.

After further testimony on other matters, the question of the selling prices of beet and cane sugar was reverted to by Mr. Fordney, and the following testimony ensued (p. 3381):

Mr. FORDNEY. And all this time Michigan sugar was sold by the Michigan Sugar Co. and all other factories in that State at 5.55.

Mr. LOWRY. Is not that because they used bad judgment?

Mr. FORDNEY. Well, they may be a pack of fools, but they are generally intelligent enough there in New York.

Mr. LOWRY. They sold out at that price because they thought it was a good figure; and I will tell you that they were blamed sorry when the market got up to 6.50 that they had sold out.

Mr. FORDNEY. No; it was when sugar was at 6.50 that they were selling it at that.

Mr. LOWRY. No; you are wrong on that.

Mr. FORDNEY. How do you know I am wrong on that? I saw their books.

Mr. LOWRY. My business, Mr. Fordney, is to sell sugar, and I keep pretty good track of what is going on.

Mr. FORDNEY. But you do not know anything about what the Michigan man's mind is, and what his contracts are, or anything about it.

Mr. LOWRY. The Michigan man is the same as a man anywhere: he wants to get the highest price he can. He sells his sugar at the highest price he can get for it, and he sells it when he thinks the market is right; and if he has misjudged the market he is very sorry.

The idea, of course, is to assume the air of virtue from the fact that the Michigan Sugar Co. misjudged the market, thereby deceiving our legislators into believing that the Michigan Sugar Co. really did something to prevent the public from paying too much for their sugar during the recent rise.

To prove my statements I refer to the following:

Under date of August 16 Messrs. Turner Bros., sugar brokers of New York City, in their daily market report stated:

"New crop beet granulated can now be purchased for October shipment on the basis of 5.55 cents cash, less 2 per cent, for shipment to Pittsburgh and points west, and basis 5.65 cents cash, less 2 per cent, for hipment to Utica, N. Y., Scranton, Pa., and points west thereof."

On that date eastern refiners were quoting granulated for immediate shipment as follows:

American Sugar Refining Co., 5.75 cents; National Sugar Refining Co., 5.85 cents; Arbuckle Bros., 5.85 cents; Federal Sugar Refining Co., 5.95 cents; Warner Sugar Refining Co., 5.85 cents; Franklin Sugar Refining Co., 5.75 cents.

W. H. Edgar & Son, sugar brokers of Detroit, state in their circular of August 18:

"In the regular beet territory (Pittsburgh, Buffalo, and west) new crop Michigan granulated is now offered for shipment after the commencement of operations at buyers' option during October basis 5.55 cents, without guarantee."

A. H. Lamborn & Co., sugar brokers of New York City, in their market report under date of August 29 state:

"Advices from the interior state that the domestic beet refiners have practically disposed of their October production, and to-day's prices have advanced to the basis of 6.05 cents."

October 12, the date Mr. Fordney refers to, was a holiday in New York, but under date of October 13 Messrs. Turner Bros., in their market review of that date, stated:

"New crop beet granulated is quoted to-day on the basis of 6.50 cents cash less 2 per cent, to Utica and Scranton and points west thereof, carrying the same eastern basis of rail freight. These sugars can be purchased for shipment in turn during November."

On that same date eastern refiners were quoting granulated for prompt shipment as follows:

American Sugar Refining Co., 6.75 cents; National Sugar Refining Co., 6.75 cents; Arbuckle Bros., 6.75 cents; Federal Sugar Refining Co., 6.75 cents; Warner Sugar Refining Co., 6.75 cents; Franklin Sugar Refining Co., 6.75 cents.

On my return to New York I wrote Congressman J. W. Fordney as follows:

NEW YORK, *December 14, 1911.*

Hon. J. W. FORDNEY,
Congressman from Michigan, Washington, D. C.

DEAR SIR: When I was on the stand last Saturday you made the claim that the Michigan Sugar Co. had sold sugar at 5.65 cents basis, when the New York refiners were quoting 6.75 cents. This I denied, stating that the Michigan factories unquestionably sold at 5.65, but they did it when the New York refiners were selling at 10 points higher, or 5.75 cents, which was some time in August. In other words, the 5.65 cents price looked so good to the Michigan Sugar Co. that they anticipated the market in August and made contracts at this figure for delivery as soon as possible, with the understanding that this would be some time in October. In this I was absolutely correct, and it is unfortunate that we did not have Mr. Hathaway's affidavit before us when we were arguing this point. Carefully reading Mr. Hathaway's statement, you will note that he does not make the claim that you did. He merely gives the price at which the sugars, delivered in fulfillment of contracts, is invoiced, making no mention as to the date the sales were made. The Michigan Sugar Co. having no philanthropic motives in mind, had simply misjudged the market and sold too soon, as I claimed. Of course I recognize that Mr. Hathaway's statement is misleading, both to you and to the public, and was intended to be so, just as his statement to the Ways and Means Committee in 1908 (which President Warren did not contradict), to the effect that the American Sugar Refining Co. had no interest in the Michigan Sugar Co. was intended to mislead them. In the present instance the Michigan Sugar Co. is trying to assume the air of virtue, from the fact that they misjudged the market. I might add that for this same reason some New York refiners in October were still delivering sugar at 5 cents, which was sold by them before the advance.

As your statements were very emphatic on the point, and as it is clear that the statement misled you, it seems to me that you should take occasion at the earliest opportunity to correct the false impression that one, not knowing the facts, would get from reading the evidence.

Respectfully, yours,

FRANK C. LOWRY.

P. S.—I am sending copies of this letter to other members of the committee.

Under date of December 16, 1911, Mr. Fordney replied as follows:

WASHINGTON, D. C., *December 16, 1911.*

Mr. FRANK C. LOWRY,
  138 Front Street, New York, N. Y.

MY DEAR SIR: Replying to yours of the 14th, would say your story, as set forth in your letter, is quite in keeping with what you have stated heretofore in my presence, and incorrect. Your figures are not correct and your conclusions are not correct. You would evidently present any argument to mislead the public to believe that free trade on sugar would inure to the benefit of the consumer, when, in fact, it would benefit only those interested in refining imported raw sugar.

The beet-sugar industry is here to stay, and I firmly believe the present rate of duty on imported raw sugar will not be disturbed for some time to come. Certainly not while the Republican Party is in power, for the Republican Party does not seem willing to swell the coffers of men engaged in refining raw sugar and to aid in the destruction of a magnificent industry, now giving aid in a most substantial manner to the consumers of sugar in the United States. I am,

Very truly, yours,

J. W. FORDNEY.

My answer to this letter follows under date of December 18:

NEW YORK, *December 18, 1911.*

Hon. J. W. FORDNEY,
  House Office Building, Washington, D. C.

DEAR SIR: I have to acknowledge your letter of December 10, and have read same with interest.

I appreciate that history shows that many statesmen have taken the easiest, if not the most honorable way, of disposing of a displeasing statement of facts made by the opposition, by the simple method of calling the man a liar, at the same time taking very good care not to attempt to prove the latter statement. If you desire to prove that every statement which I made to you in my letter of December 14 is correct, write to any broker handling Michigan beet sugars; Chicago would, perhaps, be the best market, and the largest brokers there are: Meinrath Brokerage Co., F. C. Van Ness, Chester Hogle, Wm. F. Havemeyer & Co., and in Detroit you can write to Mr. Goodlow Edgar, of Wm. H. Edgar Co. (the latter company has for many years worked hand in glove with the American Sugar Refining Co., receiving special rebates for distributing their product, etc.).

When Mr. Hathaway is brought right to the point, I do not believe that he himself will deny the statements which I have made regarding this affidavit of his, or will deny that the beet-sugar factories of Michigan this year based their selling price on the cane-sugar refiners' quotations, just as they have always done, and when they sold their sugar at 5.55 cents, 5.65 cents, and 5.75 cents, etc., the New York refiners were making sales at the usual difference, or 10 points higher than these figures. In fact, it seems to me that a careful analysis of Mr. Hathaway's affidavit shows this. He himself admits that they sold sugar as high as 6.40 cents, and an examination of their books will show that at that time they were so thoroughly sold out they had little or no sugar unsold for delivery prior to December 1.

An attempt has been made to show that the Michigan Sugar Co. sold to their customers at 5.55 cents to 5.65 cents when the New York refiners were selling at 6.75 cents. This is the statement which you made, and it is not correct. This is not a theory of mine, but a statement of facts, and can be readily proved by you if you desire to do so. I was under the impression that your statement was the result of an incorrect conclusion you had drawn from Mr. Hathaway's affidavit, which was obviously made up with the view of concealing the real facts, and with the desire to have their attitude improperly construed by the public, just as it was by you. Unless you make some effort to ascertain the facts and correct this false impression, I am forced to the conclusion that your attitude on this important matter coincides with Mr. Hathaway's.

In reply to your intimation that the public would not benefit by a reduction in the duties on raw and refined sugar, I refer to Messrs. Willett & Gray's table of refined-sugar prices for the year 1891, which I sent to Mr. Malby last week, and copy of which I inclose herewith, showing conclusively that when the tariff on sugar was removed the price of refined sugar to the consumer was reduced 1½ cents per pound in one week.

Naturally I am interested in your statement to the effect that the Republican Party will not reduce the duty on sugar while it is in power, but will continue its policy of failing to keep faith with its pledges to the people. The present sugar tariff or half the present rate can not even be defended on the illusive theory of protecting American industries to the extent of "the difference in cost of production between here and abroad." Such a course will unquestionably lead to the retirement of the Republican Party from power after March 4, 1913.

I am, respectfully, yours,   FRANK C. LOWRY.

. Receiving no reply to this letter, I again wrote Congressman J. W. Fordney, under date of January 9, as follows:

NEW YORK, *January 9, 1912.*

Hon. J. W. FORDNEY,
House of Representatives, Washington, D. C.

DEAR SIR: I have had no reply to my letter to you of December 18, 1911, and am naturally curious to know whether or not you intend correcting in the record the misstatement which you have made, regarding which we have had some correspondence.

Yours, respectfully,   FRANK C. LOWRY.

I am still without any reply to the above.

To me this example clearly shows the extent to which those who profit by high protection will go to conceal the real facts in their effort to confuse our legislators and the public generally.

I give you this simply as a matter of information.

Yours, very truly,   FRANK C. LOWRY,
           Secretary.

COMMITTEE OF WHOLESALE GROCERS,
New York, March 1, 1912.

DEAR SIR: As an indication of how incorrect is the claim that the beet-sugar producers of the United States sell their sugars at low prices for the benefit of the American consumer, I would call attention to the fact that in anticipation of higher prices the beet-sugar producers have for several weeks withdrawn their product from the market, notwithstanding the fact that about 25 per cent of the beet sugar produced in this country during the last campaign is still unsold.

The situation is well covered by Willett & Gray's Weekly Statistical Sugar Trade Journal of February 29, from which I quote as follows:

"The beet-sugar factories are still quoting 5.90 cents, less 2 per cent, and thus practically withdrawn from the general market."

Prices of the New York cane-sugar refiners are to-day on the basis of 5.80 cents.

This action of the beet-sugar factories in withdrawing their product in the hope of getting still higher prices is taken in face of the fact that prices are to-day a half a cent higher than the lowest price touched since the 1st of January and fully 2½ cents a pound above the cost of producing beet sugar.

- Based on the beet-sugar men's figures given before the Hardwick investigating committee, it was shown that beet sugar could be produced at less than 3 cents a pound, and that the average cost was 3¼ cents a pound. On the latter basis, which is known to be high, to-day's price would show the beet-sugar men a profit of about 70 per cent over their cost of production. It would, therefore, be reasonable to expect that the dividends of 33⅓ per cent paid by the Michigan Sugar Co. and 100 per cent paid by the Union Sugar Co., of California, last year would be bettered this year.

This is not a criticism of methods, but simply a desire to call attention to the fact that these gentlemen are in business to make as much money as possible, and any attempt to deny the fact only proves that the man making the claim is either not familiar with the situation or is willfully attempting to mislead.

Respectfully, yours,

F. C. LOWRY, *Secretary.*

In Mr. Hathaway's testimony, by picking out quotations in particular markets on certain dates last fall, he now endeavors to make it appear that the beet-sugar producers did not follow the usual custom of basing their price on the New York refiner's quotation plus the freight from New York to destination. I recognize that the committee is not interested in " special prices " that are made at some stated time, but is interested only in what is the custom of the trade. And it was clearly shown in the evidence taken before the Hardwick committee that the custom of the domestic producer is to base his price on the New York refiner's quotation, delivered at various destinations throughout the interior of the country. As this includes freight from seaboard to destination, it is apparent that the price in the interior is higher than at New York. The domestic beet-sugar men were very anxious to dispose of their sugars rapidly this season, because they recognized that the higher prices obtained in the fall of 1912 would not prevail after the 1st of January, 1913, when Cuban sugars would come on to the market in free supply, and for this reason they at times anticipated the market. Their position is well covered by the following market report, issued to the trade on December 6:

With the large Cuban crop staring them in the face, and the certain knowledge that as soon as this Cuban sugar became available, prices will recede rapidly, it is not surprising that the domestic beet factories are pushing the sale of their sugar, so as to dispose of as much as possible on to-day's market, rather than hold it until after the first of the year, when they will have to compete with low-priced cane sugars. Prices are therefore quite irregular.

That their judgment was correct is shown by the fact that between January 1 and 21 the price of refined sugar in New York declined 45 points. It will be observed that this decline was not due to any pressure of domestic sugar, but was due to the fact that the new Cuban crop was being harvested and was being received by our refiners at lower prices.

The following quotations are from a certain letter sent to the wholesale grocery trade of the United States by Mr. Lowry:

Quotations for granulated sugar at New York (cents per pound net cash).

	1911	1910	1909	1908	1907	1906
Average Jan. 1 to July 1	4.720	5.015	4.652	5.036	4.646	4.405
Average July 1 to Dec. 31	5.969	4.929	4.874	4.878	4.650	4.619
Average for year	5.345	4.972	4.765	4.957	4.649	4.515

WILLETT & GRAY.

Mr. Fordney. When I want you to quote prices I will ask you. I am probably quite as familiar with them as you are.

Mr. Shackleford. For the benefit of the committee, I hope only one witness will testify at a time.

The Chairman. Let him put the figures in the record for the benefit of the committee.

Mr. Lowry. I have handed them to the reporter.

Mr. Fordney. All right, put them into the record; but, at the same time, I want my question answered. Beet sugar was offered on the market on the 12th day of October, according to the testimony given before the Hardwick committee, and at $5.50 per hundred pounds——

Mr. Lowry (interposing). That——

Mr. Fordney (continuing). Let me put my question. And within a very few days thereafter refined sugar in New York dropped from 7¼ to 5.75 cents. Is that not true?

Mr. Lowry. It did drop from 7¼ to 6.75 cents.

Mr. Fordney. Is it not true that there was testimony furnished here by affidavit, as a part of the statistics of the Treasury Department, that the average price of raw imported sugar during that year and during that period was 2.74 cents in bond in New York?

Mr. Lowry. No; it was not that——

Mr. Fordney. Whereas your prices for refined sugar were quoted on prices for European raws, and there was not a pound of European raws coming into this country?

Mr. Lowry. This 1911 we are talking about——

Mr. Fordney (interposing). Is that not true?

Mr. Lowry. The average margin between raw and refined sugar in 1911, according to Willett & Gray, was $0.89 per hundred, a normal margin.

Mr. Fordney. What raws are you talking about?

Mr. Lowry. The difference between the duty-paid value of raw sugar and the refiners' selling price. That shows the margin between raw and refined for that year was nothing more than normal.

Mr. Fordney. European raws, you are talking about?

Mr. Lowry. No; the raw sugar actually received.

Mr. Fordney. Your prices for the year, you say, are based upon European raws quoted on the market and as furnished by Willett & Gray?

Mr. Lowry. I beg pardon. The price of refined sugar during that year was based upon the price that refiners were pa ng for raw sugars plus the margin which covered the cost of refining, as it always is.

Mr. Fordney. Mr. Chairman, I want to state now that in the Hardwick hearings you will find the price of refined sugar in New York in July, August, and September, 1911, was based upon European raws, and that I now file and put into this record a statement showing that the price for raws during that time was $2.74, less the duty, and yet that refined sugar sold as high as 7½ cents per pound in New York, and that when beet sugar was put on the market in October, 1911, New York refined sugar dropped to 5.75 cents.

FRANK C. LOWRY, SALES AGENT, FEDERAL SUGAR REFINING CO.

Mr. Fordney. * * * I want to know what the Federal Sugar Refining Co. sold sugars for?

Mr. Lowry. The Federal Sugar Refining Co. and other refineries on July 6 advanced their price from 5 to 5.1. * * * Now, the market advanced right on up to 6.75, and the trade kept buying on each successive advance. * * * The demand came on to us so fast we could not take care of it and we went to 7 cents. Arbuckle & Co. were delivering promptly, and they went to 7 cents. We were about 10 days oversold at the time, and Arbuckle was the only refiner prepared to give immediate delivery, and he jumped his price to 7.5. * * * We wanted to keep in the market and supply our customers right along, and we put the price at 7.25, and at 7.25 the market stopped, and from that time on, whether we talk about beet sugars or cane sugars, the market became absolutely a jobber's market. The beet-sugar price was 6.5 cents.

Mr. Lowry. Is the object of that question to show that beet-sugar men sell their sugars at a lower price than they can get for them in the market?

Mr. Fordney. They did that year, did they not?

Mr. Lowry. There never was any charity business that year, and never was in any year.

Mr. Fordney. Did they not put beet sugar on the market at $5.55 when you were selling at 7¼ cents in New York?

Mr. Lowry. No, sir.

Mr. Fordney. I say the record shows that is the testimony.

Mr. Lowry. I say the record is incorrect, then. They sold these sugars in August for $5.55, when our price was $5.65.

Mr. Fordney. I am not talking about beet sugar on the market in August, but it was in the record that way. There was no beet sugar at all put on the market in August, and——

Mr. Lowry (interposing). The price of——

Mr. Fordney (continuing). Let me take just a minute and finish my question. They put sugar on the market in October, 1911, and then when you dropped your price from 7¼ to 5.75 cents they put their sugars on the market at 5.55 cents and when you were selling at 7¼ cents. Is that not a fact?

Mr. Lowry. If you will look in the record of the Hardwick committee investigation——

Mr. Fordney (interposing). Is that not true?

Mr. Lowry. You will find that the price for domestic beet sugar followed the market as it always has and advanced or declined as world's values advanced or declined. You will find on page 3372 of the Hardwick hearings testimony to show that from the high point reached in September until the early part of December the London sugar market declined 2s. 9d., or 66 cents a hundred pounds, and that American beet sugar during the same period dropped 60 points from their high figure.

Mr. Fordney. Oh, no; they do not even belong to the same human family.

Mr. Lowry. They want the same thing.

Mr. Fordney. I repeat, they do not belong to the same human race with the refiners of sugar in New York. [Laughter.]

The Chairman. Let us have order in the room.

Mr. Lowry. Is that their misfortune?

Mr. Fordney. Mr. Lowry, you stated a few minutes ago that refined sugar sells on the Pacific coast at a higher price than in the East?

Mr. Lowry. Yes.

Mr. FORDNEY. Is it not true that the sugar imported on the Pacific coast to be refined is practically all free sugar coming into this country?

Mr. LOWRY. All sugar used on the Pacific coast is free sugar, either being domestic beet or domestic cane or Hawaiian sugar. That is what I said in my testimony.

Mr. FORDNEY. From Hawaii or the Philippines?

Mr. LOWRY. Well, from the Philippines; a trifle; not very much.

Mr. FORDNEY. That sugar is not refined by the sugar-beet men?

Mr. LOWRY. No; it is refined by the Western refinery and the C. & H. refinery. They both take advantage of the tariff in the same way.

Mr. FORDNEY. In the American Sugar Refining Co.?

Mr. LOWRY. No; I understand the American Sugar Refining Co. now state they have no interest in the Western Refining Co. They had up to about a year ago, I think; and since the American Sugar Refining Co. has no control of the Western Refining Co. it may be fair to state that they have got the price higher than for a year or so previously as compared with the New York price.

Mr. FORDNEY. According to your own statement, consumers of sugar on the Pacific coast are paying more for their sugar than consumers of sugar on the Atlantic coast, whereas raw sugar comes in free on the Pacific coast and pays a duty on the Atlantic coast?

Mr. LOWRY. They pay more for sugar that does not pay any revenue to the Government.

Mr. FORDNEY. Then, the tariff has nothing to do with the price which the consumer has to pay?

Mr. LOWRY. Yes, sir; it has everything to do with the price the consumer has to pay out there, as their price is based upon the in-bond value of foreign sugars, plus the duty and cost of refining, and not upon the cost of production.

Mr. HARRISON. Was not the effect of admitting Hawaiian sugar there merely to raise the price of Hawaiian sugar to the level of the price of sugars in this country?

Mr. LOWRY. Precisely.

Mr. HARRISON. In other words, the tariff wall was not opened up wide enough to let in enough world competition to lower the price?

Mr. LOWRY. Exactly. They just let in a small amount, and that let in took advantage of the tariff and boosted their price.

Mr. FORDNEY. If that were the case and you put sugar on the free list, the consumer on the Atlantic coast would not get any advantage; you would just hold up the price?

Mr. LOWRY. Mr. Fordney, there are any number of gentlemen in this room representing the domestic industry who are prepared to testify that if you take the duty off sugar there will be a corresponding reduction in the price of sugar to the consumer, and that is why they don't want it done. If you will refer to the Hardwick Committee Hearings, pages 3547 and 3554, you will find that Mr. Willett, of Willett & Gray, gave a very clear example of the effect of the tariff on the price of sugar. He stated:

All the analyses of changing from duty to free sugar show that whenever duty is taken off the cost of refining decreases, and when the duty is added the cost of refining increases, but these analyses also show that whenever duty is taken off the consumer gets the full benefit of the amount of duty taken off and also a part of the lower cost of refining, and whenever the duty is increased the refiners bear a certain portion of the increase and the consumer does not pay the full addition of the duty.

And on page 3554 the following passage occurs:

I would like to have the committee satisfied that any reduction of the duty goes to the consumer and any addition of the duty is paid by the consumer in any year under any duty which differs from any other duty, making necessary allowances for market fluctuation affected by supply and demand.

Mr. FORDNEY. I was simply following out the logic of your contention and not stating what I believed. But just let me ask you a question along that line: When you had the opportunity, when you had a clear field, when there was no domestic beet or cane sugar on the market in 1911, in what way did you apply your philanthropic ideas to the consumer?

Mr. LOWRY. We never had a clear field in the selling of sugars. What difference does it make whether we compete with cane or beet sugar?

Mr. FORDNEY. You stated a few minutes ago that because of the higher cost of production of beet sugar a higher duty was demanded by manufacturers of beet and cane sugars?

Mr. LOWRY. That seems to be the object of putting the cost high.

Mr. FORDNEY. Has it not been shown here that since the beet-sugar industry began in this country the cost of production has been materially lowered?

Mr. LOWRY. And their profits materially increased—correspondingly increased.

Mr. FORDNEY. That is not what I asked you. I asked you if the cost of production has not been materially lowered.

Mr. LOWRY. I should think it would be; and here we have an indication of the domestic producers' greed. Ten years ago they urged that if they could only have 10 years of the present basis of tariff bounty they would be prepared to work under lower tariff rates. They have had those 10 years and, although we find them much fatter than 10 years ago, they still stick their forefeet comfortably in the tariff trough and are unwilling to make any concession to the consumer by removing even one of those feet, notwithstanding the fact that even you admit that during this period they have very materially reduced their cost of operation.

Mr. FORDNEY. Is it not true that every particle of legislation since that time affecting sugar has been to lower the tariff on sugar?

Mr. LOWRY. Well, there has been practically no legislation to lower the tariff since the bill of 1897, with the exception of 20 per cent rate on Cuban sugars, a part of which the Cubans get and a part of which the consumer in the United States gets.

Mr. FORDNEY. Mr. Lowry, let me——

Mr. LOWRY (interposing). On this point let me say——

Mr. FORDNEY (continuing). Let me get this straight while I am at it——

Mr. LOWRY. This clears it up——

Mr. FORDNEY (continuing). It is true that since the sugar-beet industry began in this country the duty on sugar from Cuba has been lowered 20 per cent?

Mr. LOWRY. Yes.

Mr. FORDNEY. Is it not also true that Porto Rican sugar comes in free since that time?

Mr. LOWRY. Yes.

Mr. FORDNEY. Is it not further true that Philippine sugar comes in free since that time?

Mr. LOWRY. Up to 300,000 tons.

Mr. FORDNEY. So that it is true, as I stated in my former question, that every particle of legislation affecting the duty on sugar since the beginning of the beet-sugar industry in this country has been to lower the duty and increase competition with free sugar or sugar bearing lower rates?

Mr. LOWRY. The legislation has been toward giving the Philippines, Hawaii, and Porto Rico the benefit of our high tariff wall.

Mr. FORDNEY. Even if you prefer to put it that way, that is all of the legislation there has been affecting sugar, so that my statement is true, is it not?

Mr. LOWRY. We were talking a few minutes ago about the price of sugar——

The CHAIRMAN. If you will allow me to suggest right there, Mr. Fordney, do not overlook the fact that the American flag is floating over Hawaii, and that legislation affecting her production of sugar is not in fact a lowering of the tariff wall.

Mr. FORDNEY. And I want to say to the chairman that we got sugar from Hawaii long prior to the period when the American flag began to fly over Hawaii.

The CHAIRMAN. I understand, but Hawaii is a part of this country, and in speaking of Hawaiian sugar coming in free, I thought your statement might be misunderstood.

Mr. FORDNEY. I am not referring to Hawaii, or at least I did not bring it up; the witness did.

Mr. LOWRY. As an indication of the effect on the market of beet sugar, which comes on the market in the fall, let us take the prices for the last six months and the first six months of the following years and compare them:

1911:
Average from January to July_____ $4.72 per 100 pounds.
Average from July to December_____ $5.96 per 100 pounds.
Average for the year_____ $5.34 per 100 pounds.

Which was higher, as you will notice, during the last six months.

1910:
Average from January to July_____ $5.05 per 100 pounds.
Average from July to December_____ $4.92 per 100 pounds.
1909:
Average from January to July_____ $4.65 per 100 pounds.
Average from July to December_____ $4.87 per 100 pounds.
Average for the year_____ $4.76 per 100 pounds.
1908: Average from January to July——

Mr. FORDNEY. To expedite matters you can put that in the record.

Mr. LOWRY. I believe it is in. It shows that for the six years compared three of the years sugar was higher during the last six months and during three years it was a trifle lower. It shows that beet sugar follows the markets of the world.

Mr. FORDNEY. Is it not true that domestic beet sugar sold in New York this fall cheaper than your price?

. . Mr. LOWRY. Yes, and cheaper than it did in Colorado. It sold in Colorado for 5.20, whereas it was shipped to New York and paid freight charges 80 cents and there sold for 4.6 cents per pound.

Mr. FORDNEY. It sold for a less price in New York than you were selling your sugar for, and you were obliged to close your factory on account of it?

Mr. LOWRY. No; not at all.

Mr. FORDNEY. Did you not stop sales?

Mr. LOWRY. No; why, gracious me, no. They have sold—oh, well, I don't know how many carloads they have sold—but certainly not enough to close our factory. But when the people of Colorado were paying a higher price they——

Mr. FORDNEY (interposing). Just answer my question. I know you very well.

Mr. LOWRY. I expect you do.

Mr. FORDNEY. You are wound up for all time to come. When you sold sugar for 4.90 cents in New York the domestic beet sugar undersold you this fall, did it not?

Mr. LOWRY. They have to or they would not sell it at all.

Mr. FORDNEY. Did they not do it?

Mr. LOWRY. Yes, 10 cents per hundred. You know that beet sugar never sells for the price received for cane sugar, because the trade will not pay the same price for it.

Mr. FORDNEY. Oh, my friend——

Mr. LOWRY (interposing). You understand that that is so?

Mr. FORDNEY. I understand that you are a very resourceful arguer. [Laughter.]

Mr. LOWRY. Thank you.

Mr. FORDNEY. You stated in your remarks a few minutes ago that the production of sugar in Louisiana was a great detriment to the people there, I believe?

Mr. LOWRY. I say that that is the statement many people in Louisiana make.

Mr. FORDNEY. The statement was made before the Hardwick committee by a gentleman from Louisiana that more than half of the people of the State of Louisiana were now directly engaged in the production either of cane or cane sugar?

Mr. LOWRY. I do not know anything about their statements on the subject.

Mr. FORDNEY. Well, that was the testimony.

Mr. LOWRY. But I do know that the claim is made that Louisiana would be far better off if they would cut the area of the State up into small farms and get away from the big-plantation idea and produce other crops.

Mr. FORDNEY. That is the claim of the free trader, is it not, and not of the sugar grower or manufacturer down there?

Mr. LOWRY. No, sir; that is the claim of people in Louisiana who have no interest in the matter so far as I know.

Mr. FORDNEY. You never heard a man engaged in the production of cane sugar in Louisiana make that statement?

Mr. LOWRY. No; not any man engaged in the production of cane sugar, but by people there who know the conditions. Yes; I have heard people in the business say so, but they were not engaged in production of cane sugar.

Mr. FORDNEY. Are you secretary and treasurer of this Wholesale Grocers' Association yet?

Mr. LOWRY. Yes, sir.

Mr. FORDNEY. You stated before the Hardwick committee that there were no fees or annual dues or dues of any kind charged to members of your association?

Mr. LOWRY. Yes, sir; and the situation is precisely the same as when I stated it to the Hardwick committee and to the Finance Committee of the Senate.

Mr. FORDNEY. None collected from the members of that association?

Mr. LOWRY. That is right. They contribute work only.

Mr. FORDNEY. You stated that there was never a meeting held of even two or three members of the committee?

Mr. LOWRY. No; but there have been meetings, as I see these people frequently.

Mr. FORDNEY. I know that you represent them and write them and go around and see them occasionally.

Mr. LOWRY. Yes, sir.

Mr. FORDNEY. So that there is a meeting of at least two members when you and another fellow are together? [Laughter.]

Mr. LOWRY. I think that is correct.

The CHAIRMAN. Order, gentlemen.

Mr. FORDNEY. You stated further to the Hardwick committee that the only money you had ever had contributed for this effort to secure free sugar had been given by Mr. Spreckles, president of the Federal Sugar Refining Co., some $12,000?

Mr. LOWRY. Yes, sir.

Mr. FORDNEY. Does that continue?

Mr. LOWRY. Yes, sir; no change in the situation.

Mr. FORDNEY. So that all of the money produced for your use in advertising comes from the Federal Sugar Refining Co., or its president; is that right?

Mr. LOWRY. Yes, sir; that is right. And right here I will put into the record a statement that I gave to Chairman Hardwick of the Special Committee Investigating the American Sugar Refining Co., and which he incorporated in his speech, showing exactly who our committee was, what it was, and what it stood for.

Mr. HARDWICK. Mr. Chairman, before I proceed to a discussion of another branch of this question, I wish to insert in the record, as a matter of simple justice to him, a letter from a gentleman who has been previously assailed in this debate by opponents of this bill, and who has been severely criticised all over the country by the beneficiaries of the sugar tax. It seems to me that these gentlemen think that it is perfectly proper for any gentleman to favor a retention of duties for the "protection" of the industry in which he is interested and conduct as active and as aggressive a propaganda to save his "protection" as he may desire, but that it is hardly short of a crime for anybody who speaks for the millions of American consumers and urges a reduction of tariff burdens to conduct a propaganda in support of that view. The gentleman to whom I refer has, in my judgment, done a great work for the people of the country by his aggressive and forceful advocacy of the removal of the duty on sugar, and while he has necessarily earned the ill will of the protected interest, because of his aggressive fight, he is undoubtedly entitled to the gratitude and the good will of every American consumer who has a grocery bill to pay. I refer to Mr. Frank C. Lowry, of New York, sales agent for the Federal Sugar Refining Co., and secretary of the committee of wholesale grocers, and I invite the attention of the committee to the letter from him, which follows:

NEW YORK, *March 18, 1912.*

Hon. THOMAS W. HARDWICK,
Chairman Special Committee on Investigation of
The American Sugar Refining Co. and others,
House of Representatives, Washington, D. C.

MY DEAR SIR: Those opposed to any reduction in the tariff on sugar have endeavored to besmirch the standing of the Committee of Wholesale Grocers, of which I have served as secretary, because I am also in charge of the sales department of the Federal Sugar Refining Co., an independent refinery. There has at no time been any mystery as to who I was or where I stood on this important matter. Certainly I was very glad to have the opportunity to state it clearly to your committee when I appeared before them last July. The Wholesale Grocers' Committee was formed in 1909 for the purpose, as stated on our letterheads, of "obtaining cheaper sugar for consumers through reduction of duties on raw and refined sugars." I believed in the principle advocated, was instrumental in forming this committee, and have served as its secretary without any remuneration, direct or indirect, because the other members desired it. My name, and that of the other members of the committee, has appeared on all our stationery. We have been particularly careful about this, so that all might know exactly who was behind the movement. Had there been any desire on my part or that of the other members of the committee to conceal the fact that I was interested in this work, this would not have been done.

With the exception of myself all our members are actively engaged in the wholesale grocery business. They are: Carl Schuster, Koenig & Schuster, New York City; W. H. Baker, Baker & Co., Winchester, Va.; B. F. Persons, Patsone & Scoville Co., Evansville, Ind.; H. C. Beggs, Dilworth Bros. & Co., Pittsburgh, Pa.; R. E. Collins, Collins & Co., Birmingham, Ala.; A. S. Hammond, Monypeny-Hammond Co., Columbus, Ohio; G. Thalheimer, Syracuse, N. Y.; Henry Baden, Henry Baden & Co., Independence, Kans.; F. J. Dessoir, R. C. Williams & Co., New York City; H. T. Gates, E. W. Gates & Co., Richmond, Va.; W. E. Small, the A. B. Small Co., Macon, Ga.; E. L. Woodward, E. L. Woodward & Co., Norfolk, Va.; A. Blanton, A. Blanton Grocery Co., Marion, N. C.; Jacob Zinsmeister, J. Zinsmeister & Bro., Louisville, Ky.; A. Brinkley, A. Brinkley & Co., Norfolk, Va.; R. E. Bentley, Bentley, Shriver & Co., Baltimore, Md.; John E. Talmadge, jr., Talmadge Bros. & Co., Athens, Ga.: Isaac Horner, Henry Horner & Co., Chicago, Ill.; Edward Cumpson, T. & E. Cumpson, Buffalo, N. Y.; E. P. McKinney, McKinney & Co., Binghamton, N. Y.; H. Y. McCord, McCord-Stuart Co., Atlanta, Ga.; A. S. Webster, Webster Grocery Co., Danville, Ill.

These gentlemen are from 14 different States, and the firms represented have a total rating of nearly $8,000,000.

In the work we have been doing we have had the cooperation of a great many wholesale and retail grocery houses that are not members of the committee, but who would be glad to become members of it were it desirable to have the number increased. Furthermore, I am firmly convinced that 90 per cent of the wholesale grocery trade of the country is in sympathy with our efforts. The National Wholesale Grocers' Association, as an organization, has not taken any action regarding the tariff on sugar, for the reason, as they have repeatedly stated, "As an organization we do not deal with political questions of any kind." They leave matters of this kind to be dealt with separately by the various local organizations and individual members, and the petitions now filed with the Ways and Means Committee show how thoroughly this has been done. I might mention, however, that the National Canners' Association, with a membership of over 3,000 firms, does not feel this way about it, but passed resolutions favoring a lower duty on sugar, and have instructed the chairman of their committee on legislation, Mr. Bert N. Fernald, to use his best efforts to bring about such a reduction. The National Bottlers' Protective Association have acted in a similar way, the only difference being that their resolution calls for "free sugar."

Previous to the time this committee was formed, in 1909, the general public knew little regarding the details of the sugar tariff, and all our efforts have been along the lines of publishing the facts, feeling satisfied that if the people were informed what the tax was and its effect they would demand and receive the relief from the excessive rate to which they are clearly entitled. As a result of our efforts thousands of petitions asking for a reduction in the tariff on sugar have been sent to Congressmen, signed by individuals, firms, corporations, granges, civic associations, etc. Through these the signers have spoken for themselves and others who are in sympathy with the movement. These are the people who will hold their Congressman responsible for what he does or does not do to secure a lower tax rate on sugar.

To distribute this information, besides requiring effort on the part of this committee, required funds, and the Federal Sugar Refining Co. has helped us financially. Investigation by your committee disclosed that the Federal Sugar Refining Co. was absolutely independent, having no affiliation, directly or indirectly, with the Sugar Trust. Consequently their interest in the lower duties is identical with that of the consumer. A lower tariff rate will reduce the price of sugar, resulting in an increased consumption, so that a larger business can be done at a reduced expense.

The American Sugar Refining Co. is clearly on record as desiring no change in the present tariff, as reference to the Payne-Aldrich tariff hearings of 1909, pages 3430–3440, will disclose a letter and a brief filed by them, urging that the present tariff rate be maintained. Thus the line is clearly established with consumers, manufacturers, dealers, and independent refiners desiring lower duties, and opposed to this is the Sugar Trust and their allies, the domestic sugar producers.

As this committee think it should be clearly stated exactly who we are and also that the work we have done has been because we believe in the principles advocated, and for no other reason, we would appreciate if you can arrange to have this printed in the record.

Very respectfully, yours,

FRANK C. LOWRY, *Secretary.*

Mr. FORDNEY. Why, there is not a Congressman nor a dealer in the country to-day who has not got a copy of that.

Mr. LOWRY. I am glad to know that, because I have certainly been engaged in an effort to get it into their possession.

Mr. FORDNEY. Why, of course. You send it out with practically every barrel of sugar or package of sugar that you send out, unless the purchaser objects to it.

Mr. LOWRY. No; that list was never sent out with any sugar.

Mr. FORDNEY. You send out letters, do you not, and make appeals for free sugar?

Mr. LOWRY. We send out statements showing it would be to the interest of the consumer; yes.

Mr. FORDNEY. That is, that in your opinion it would be?

Mr. LOWRY. Well, we can not do any more than that.

Mr. FORDNEY. Mr. Lowry, you stated that the labor cost in the production of sugar has nothing to do with the cost of sugar?

Mr. LOWRY. I say that the price of domestic sugar is not arrived at by taking their bases of cost and adding a fair margin to it.

Mr. FORDNEY. No; you did not say that.

Mr. LOWRY. Well, I will read what I said.

Mr. FORDNEY. Well, I would rather have the clerk to read it.

Mr. LOWRY. Let the clerk read it. He took it from the printed pamphlet, I believe.

Mr. FORDNEY. I will waive that point.

Mr. LOWRY. You are so unsuspicious when the beet-sugar man is on the stand that I am surprised you should be so suspicious now.

Mr. FORDNEY. I am suspicious of you and know you.

Mr. LOWRY. Yes; and I have proved several of your statements incorrect.

Mr. FORDNEY. I have had from you a volume of this stuff you are putting into the record. I could not read it in a week if I were to make a great effort, there is so much of it. You are all right and very proper, and fighting hard for free sugar. You have your reasons therefor. Now, then, you stated that the labor cost in the production of beet sugar practically had nothing to do with the price at which that sugar was sold?

Mr. LOWRY. I said it was a very small item in the cost of production.

Mr. FORDNEY. Why, does it not take labor to raise beets and to convert beets into sugar, and is not the same thing true of cane?

Mr. LOWRY. I said in the factory. You settled the farming end of it when you put beets on the 10 per cent basis. You admitted beets as a farmer's product needed a protection of only 10 per cent, and I object only to the factory receiving over 70 per cent protection as it does under the present rate.

Mr. FORDNEY. Which " you " are you speaking of now?

Mr. LOWRY. I speak of " you " as yourself and the party you represent, the Republican Party. On this matter you personally urged that. I am not sure about it, but you can say whether it is true or not.

Mr. FORDNEY. If you knew all about it you knew that that is not so.

Mr. LOWRY. You did not——

Mr. FORDNEY (interposing). If you knew all about it you know that the rate fixed in the House was 25 per cent, the same as the Dingley law, on edible vegetables, and was lowered in the Senate.

Mr. LOWRY. I see. I thought perhaps you had something to do with those conferences, but it is immaterial. It does not make any difference. The correctness of their judgment has been proven.

Mr. FORDNEY. I did. I was on the conference committee; yes, sir. Is it not true that wages both in the beet fields and in the sugar factories of this country are much higher than they are in Europe—in Germany and France, for instance?

Mr. LOWRY. That might be an argument if this was true for paying the farmer more, but the farmer does not get more.

Mr. FORDNEY. The farmer does not get more what?

Mr. LOWRY. The farmer does not get more for his beets than the farmer in Germany does.

Mr. FORDNEY. I know that you filed with the Hardwick committee, and to end this argument I will explain that you stated the farmer in Germany got more per ton for his beets than the farmer in this country got for his beets in general. You had in mind the cooperative plan——

Mr. LOWRY (interposing). No; I did not.

Mr. FORDNEY. If you did not you do not know all about it?

Mr. LOWRY. Well, I will file the German statistics on the subject.

Mr. FORDNEY. All right. There are German statistics in the Hardwick committee hearings, and the average price received for beets by the German farmer during the period 1905–1911 was $4.45 per ton——

Mr. LOWRY. Oh, no; or that may be the case where the farmer sold his beets for $4.45 per ton and afterwards got something on the cooperative basis.

Mr. FORDNEY. Wait a minute, and let me finish——

Mr. LOWRY. We do not have to argue on that; here are the statistics.

The CHAIRMAN. Just file those statistics.

Mr. LOWRY. I also have statistics showing the prices in 1911. In our own country our farmers got $5.50 per ton and the German farmer $5.54. The German statistics show that the price for sugar beets in Germany last year averaged $6.07 per long ton.

The CHAIRMAN. Just place those in the record with your remarks.

Mr. LOWRY. All right. So that there could be no possible question on this subject, I have secured and have before me the quarterly book of statistics of the German Empire, issued by the Imperial Bureau of Statistics. This you can procure by writing to any of the United States consuls in Germany. It shows that the average price paid the farmer for sugar beets in Germany for the years 1909–10 was $5.29 per long ton; for 1910–11, $5.44; 1911–12, $6.07. F. O. Licht, the recognized sugar statistician in Europe, advises me that " conditions in other European beet-sugar countries did not differ much from those in Germany," and states that " we might add for your information that the beet growers in Europe receive other returns for their beets besides cash, viz, they are furnished with beet seed free of charge " (in the United States the farmer buys his beet seed from the factory) " they receive allowances for freight and get 40 to 60 per cent of the pulp returned to them without charge." In the United States no pulp is returned to the farmer without charge, but this by-product of the factories is sold to the farmer and nets the factory a very nice return. I would call your attention to the fact that our own Department of Agriculture in their annual report estimates the average value of sugar beets to the farmer in the United States for 1911–12 at $5.50 per short ton. As the beet-sugar factories in the United States may tell you that they are now paying much more for their sugar beets than formerly, I would call your attention to the fact that the sugar content of the beets in the United States is greater than it formerly was, and also to the fact that prices for sugar beets in Germany have also advanced. According to the German statistics the average price in Germany for 1900 was $4.76 per long ton, by which it will be noted that the average for the 1912 crop was $1.31 over the price paid in 1900, showing a greater advance than in the United States.

Mr. FORDNEY. Is it not true that filed with the Hardwick committee there were statistics, furnished by the German Government, for a period of 10 years, as I remember, but at any rate for 8 or 10 years, showing that the average price paid by the factories in Germany was $4.45; and were there not similar statistics as to France, showing the French factories paid $4.05 per ton? And except——

Mr. LOWRY. I do not know of any such statistics, but if so they were wrong.

Mr. FORDNEY. Mr. Chairman, I insist that the gentleman let me finish my question. Except where the farmer was a stockholder in a factory, and then he sold his beets at a given price, and when the dividends were paid, in order to get around payment of the corporation tax, they paid him an additional sum for his beets, which was, in fact, a profit on the business. That is the evidence before the Hardwick committee.

Mr. LOWRY. I do not know of any such statement.

Mr. FORDNEY. And in the same time in the United States the price paid for beets per ton was $5.50 to $6.91 per ton delivered at the factory. That is as far as I wish to go with you.

Mr. Lowry. Mr. Chairman, how much time have we taken? These other witnesses want to be heard.

The Chairman. Just one hour of your time has been consumed. Of course we have to take out the time consumed on cross-examination.

Mr. Lowry. We would stay here a week at that rate.

Mr. Fordney. By the way, Mr. Lowry, you said the capitalization of the sugar-beet factories was largely water?

Mr. Lowry. I did.

Mr. Fordney. Is there anything that has more watered stock than the concern you represent, the Federal Sugar Refining Co.?

Mr. Lowry. Yes, sir; and you must bear in mind that the Federal Sugar Refining Co. is not here for the purpose of asking that American consumers of sugar be taxed so that it may earn dividends on any of its stock. That is not the case as to the beet-sugar companies.

Mr. Fordney. Wait a minute there. You are here attacking the sugar-beet industry, to ask that they be not protected to earn dividends on large blocks of watered stock, as you say. Your testimony before the Hardwick committee was that you had some $3,200,000 paid in, out of a capital of $10,000,000?

Mr. Lowry. What is the purpose of that line of questioning?

Mr. Fordney. I am trying to show that the beet-sugar men could not be more greatly watered than your concern is admitted to be.

Mr. Lowry. What has that to do with the tariff?

Mr. Fordney. That is what I say, but why did you mention it if it does not have anything to do with the tariff. You made the point.

Mr. Lowry. It has a great deal to do in the beet-sugar man's case. He is asking for the privilege of taxing the American consumer for his special benefit, so that he may pay dividends on this excessive capitalization. The Federal Sugar Refining Co. is not. They come to you frankly and say that they are willing to work without any protection and meet nonbounty-fed competition from anywhere in the world. Isn't that it?

Mr. Fordney. I am not the witness—you are.

Mr. Lowry. I do not know about that.

Mr. Fordney. Can you state a single instance where there is more watered stock in the beet-sugar industry than you testified there was in your concern? If so, I would like to have you do it. Two-thirds of your stock is water.

Mr. Lowry. Right here I will file a statement showing the capitalization and daily slicing capacity of the various beet-sugar factories in the country. I call attention to the fact that the cost of erecting a beet-sugar factory is based on $1,000 per ton slicing capacity.

Name of company.	Location of plants.	Capitalization (including bonded debt).	Daily slicing capacity.
			Tons.
Alameda Sugar Co.	Alvarado, Cal.	$1,500,000	750
Anaheim Sugar Co.	Anaheim, Cal.	850,000	750
American Beet Sugar Co.	Oxnard, Cal.	20,000,000	2,000
	Chino, Cal.		700
	Lamar, Colo.		400
	Las Animas, Colo.		800
	Rocky Ford, Colo.		1,000
	Grand Island, Nebr.		400

Name of company.	Location of plants.	Capitalization (including bonded debt).	Daily slicing capacity.
			Tons.
Amalgamated Sugar Co.	Ogden, Utah.	$4,000,000	500
	Logan, Utah.		500
	Burley, Idaho.		500
Billings Sugar Co.	Billings, Mont.	1,250,000	1,650
Continental Sugar Co.	Fremont, Ohio.	2,400,000	500
	Findlay, Ohio.		600
	Blissfield, Mich.		700
Corcoran Sugar Co.	Corcoran, Cal.	1,200,000	600
	Loveland, Colo.		1,800
	Greeley, Colo.		900
	Eaton, Colo.		1,000
	Fort Collins, Colo.		1,800
Great Western Sugar Co.	Longmont, Colo.	30,000,000	1,800
	Windsor, Colo.		900
	Sterling, Colo.		800
	Brush, Colo.		900
	Fort Morgan, Colo.		700
German-American Sugar Co.	Paulding, Ohio.	2,000,000	900
	Bay City, Mich.		1,400
Holland-St. Louis Sugar Co.	Holland, Mich.	3,300,000	500
	St. Louis, Mich.		600
	Decatur, Ind.		1,000
	Swink, Colo.		1,200
Holly Sugar Co.	Holly, Colo.	5,500,000	600
	Huntington Beach, Cal.		600
Iowa Sugar Co.	Waverly, Iowa.	550,000	500
Lewiston Sugar Co.	Lewiston, Utah.	1,200,000	650
Los Alamitos.	Los Alamitos, Cal.	1,000,000	900
	Bay City, Mich.		1,300
	Caro, Mich.		1,200
Michigan Sugar Co.	Alma, Mich.	12,500,000	850
	Sebewaing, Mich.		600
	Carrollton, Mich.		900
	Crosswell, Mich.		600
Menominee River Sugar Co.	Menominee, Mich.	825,000	1,000
Minnesota Sugar Co.	Chaska, Minn.	1,200,000	600
Mount Clemens Sugar Co.	Mount Clemens, Mich.	600,000	600
Chippewa Sugar Co.	Chippewa Falls, Wis.	700,000	600
Nevada Sugar Co.	Fallon, Nev.	1,000,000	600
Owosso Sugar Co.	Owosso, Mich.	2,300,000	1,000
	Lansing, Mich.		600
Pope, Charles.	Riverdale, Ill.	500,000	600
Rock Country Sugar Co.	Janesville, Wis.	800,000	600
Sacramento Valley Sugar Co.	Hamilton City, Cal.	2,210,000	700
Santa Ana Cooperative.	Dyer, Cal.	1,000,000	600
San Joaquim Valley Sugar Co.	Visalia, Cal.	1,225,000	350
Scottsbluff Sugar Co.	Scottsbluff, Nebr.	1,200,000	1,200
National Sugar Manufacturing Co.	Sugar City, Colo.	1,500,000	500
San Luis Valley Sugar Co.	Monte Vista, Colo.	1,500,000	600
Southern California Sugar Co.	Santa Ana, Cal.	1,000,000	750
Spreckels Sugar Co.	Spreckels, Cal.	5,000,000	3,000
Toledo Sugar Co.	Rossford, Ohio.	1,000,000	1,200
Union Sugar Co.	Betteravia, Cal.	3,000,000	800
United Sugar & Land Co.	Garden City, Kans.	8,000,000	900
	Lehigh, Utah.		1,200
	Garland, Utah.		750
	Austin, Utah.		500
Utah-Idaho Sugar Co.	Idaho Falls, Idaho.	11,000,000	750
	Sugar, Idaho.		800
	Blackfoot, Idaho.		650
	Nampa, Idaho.		600
Southwestern Sugar & Land Co.	Glendale, Ariz.	3,400,000	600
United States Sugar Co.	Madison, Wis.	550,000	600
Washington State Sugar Co.	Waverly, Wash.	500,000	500
West Bay City Sugar Co.	West Bay City, Mich.	200,000	900
West Michigan Sugar Co.	Charlevoix, Mich.	350,000	600
Western Sugar & Land Co.	Grand Junction, Colo.	2,000,000	500
Wisconsin Sugar Co.	Menominee Falls, Wis.	1,500,000	600
Western Sugar Refining Co.	Marine City, Mich.	100,000	550
Total.		141,410,000	63,550

Mr. FORDNEY. You said the duty you recommend on sugar is higher than the duty collected by foreign countries generally?

Mr. LOWRY. Yes.

Mr. FORDNEY. The duty you recommend?

Mr. Lowry. The duty that gives a certain bounty——

Mr. Fordney (interposing). Let me get this right. I understood you to say that the duty you would recommend be placed on sugar, which is a reduction, is a higher rate than that collected by lots of foreign countries on imported sugar?

Mr. Lowry. That " collected " is higher than the " protective " rate. It is a favorite trick of the sugar growers and sugar men asking for protection down here. They add the consumption tax and the import tax together and then say this import tax of other countries as compared with our own is higher.

Mr. Fordney. Mr. Lowry——

Mr. Lowry. If I might finish. For example, the import tariff in Germany is 47 cents on raw sugar and 52 cents on refined. The consumption tax in Germany is $1.50.

Mr. Fordney. On what?

Mr. Lowry. On all sugars.

Mr. Fordney. On domestic and imported?

Mr. Lowry. Yes; so that on foreign sugars imported at 47 cents add $1.50, or a total of $1.97. But the domestic sugars must also pay the $1.50 tax, so that the protective rate is only a rate of 47 cents; and that was the rate arrived at by the Brussels convention as a proper protective rate.

Mr. Shackleford. There is a difference between the consumption tax and the import tax, and both apply?

Mr. Lowry. Yes, sir.

Mr. Fordney. Does domestic sugar produced in Germany pay a tax?

Mr. Lowry. They pay the consumption tax.

Mr. Fordney. All sugar pays the consumption tax?

Mr. Lowry. Yes, sir.

Mr. Fordney. Whether domestic or imported?

Mr. Lowry. Yes, sir.

Mr. Fordney. That is your opinion?

Mr. Lowry. Yes, sir; that is a fact.

Mr. Fordney. The protection is 53 cents and not $1.98?

Mr. Lowry. Fifty-two cents on refined and 47 cents on raw.

Mr. Fordney. All right.

The Chairman. Mr. Lowry, do you desire to file briefs for witnesses on your side of the question?

Mr. Lowry. I presume they would like to file them right now. I suppose these other gentlemen may be heard if they want to?

The Chairman. Yes, you have consumed 1 hour and 10 minutes of your two hours' time allotted.

O

CPSIA information can be obtained
at www.ICGtesting.com
Printed in the USA
BVHW090930201118
533624BV00021B/1033/P